Can't Stop Won't Stop

Delorean Andrews

BK
ROYSTON
Publishing

BK Royston Publishing
P. O. Box 4321
Jeffersonville, IN 47131
502-802-5385
http://www.bkroystonpublishing.com
bkroystonpublishing@gmail.com

Cover Design: Elite Book Covers
Cover Photo:

ISBN-13: 978-1-951941-84-0

Printed in the United States of America

Dedication

To my father, Darrell who is the most humble man I have ever known. Thank you for allowing me to make my mark on the world and I refuse to let your legacy be lost. I never told you but I have always been proud of the fact that you played the bass. Rest in Paradise Pop.

To my mother Delaine. You taught me everything I know about money, real estate and business. Watching you when I was a kid motivated me to be successful. You encouraged me to develop a strong work ethic and taught me the value of money. I always joke with you by saying "Thank you for finding my father attractive" because that's why I am here today enjoying this journey through life.

Acknowledgements

I want to thank my Lord and Savior Jesus Christ for giving me the gift of intestinal fortitude and resilience.

I would like to thank my partner in crime, Desiree, for keeping me grounded and reminding me to put God first in everything I do.

Thank you to my grandmother, Ms. Annette Andrews for always praying for me and protecting me growing up. You showed me the meaning of unconditional love and helped to groom me into a responsible man.

To my dad who is in heaven smiling from ear to ear that his eldest son is continuing his legacy.

Thank you to my wonderful publishing team for the patience, excellent and professionalism that has been much appreciated in this journey to this book being constructed. Thank you, Mrs. Julia.

A special thanks to Pastor Jerome of Seeds of Greatness Bible Church for always being a listening ear and giving me wise biblical counsel.

Table of Contents

Introduction

This book was written while experiencing some of the most difficult times of my life. Between a debilitating injury, financial crisis, and failing relationship, life was looking quite grim. I was in a dark place and the only way I was going to survive was to find the motivation from within to stay the course. During this time, I began writing quotes to myself and I would reread often.

Now, I give the gift of inspiration to my readers.

You become
who you
hang around
most.
Know who you
are at all times.

Time doesn't wait for man, woman, or child. Therefore, don't put off what you can do today for tomorrow. Be wise with your time and treat it as precious as you treat your money.

Build success one brick at a time, and don't rush it. If your foundation isn't right, all the hard work you've done will be all for nothing.

Always give
from the heart,
and don't ever
expect anything
in return.

Always believe
you're great
even before
anyone else
believes it.

Every day when
you wake up,
focus all your
energy towards
becoming the
ideal version of
yourself.

Money isn't everything, so recognize that you are the gift. Your time is the most valuable resource you have.

How are you following him or her, and are they dead last?

Leaders are in a
position of power,
influence, or
authority.
Therefore, set an
example of
humbleness and
selflessness.

When I host business meetings, I have everyone sit at the round table, instead of me at the head, because we're all equal. No one man or woman is better than the next.

Don't allow people to tell you that you can't be or do something. Be a trendsetter not a trend follower.

The best place to
start is with you.
Make yourself
laugh today and
treat yourself to a
nice cup of coffee
or hot honey tea.

Brothers, there's no retirement pension waiting for you in selling drugs. Invest in yourself through education, a career, and using your gifts and talents.

Not having purpose
for all that you do,
is like driving
down the road with
no headlights in the
pitch-black
darkness.

A man without a
plan, is a man with
no future.

Don't make any
moves without your
God's approval.

To live a hundred years on this earth is a blessing, but to live a hundred years and touch hundreds of lives is better.

The tougher the
moment, the calmer
and more focused
you should
become.

I don't see myself
being special. I just
see myself having
more
responsibilities than
the next man.

In a negative world, be successful.

Why take the road everyone else has traveled? Be bold and explore the road less traveled.

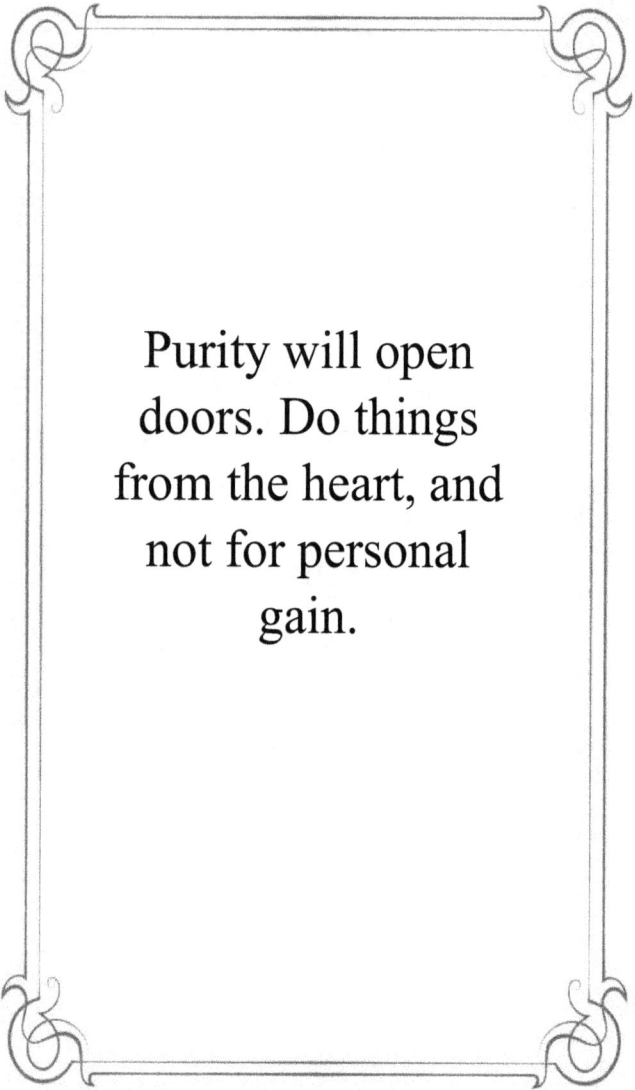

Purity will open doors. Do things from the heart, and not for personal gain.

The world doesn't owe you anything, but you owe yourself the chance to live out your dreams.

When you get a
second chance,
live each day like
you won't wake
up tomorrow. So,
for me, it's simply
how many lives
did I touch before
my funeral.

You hold the
power to change.
Don't lose who
you are. Own
what you have or
don't have.

Sometimes hitting rock bottom is the best place to start to rebuild. That way you can build a strong foundation.

Never try to build
something you
want to last on
sand or water.

People often ask me "How can you be so positive about everything?" I simply say, "Because I saw everything negative my entire life."

A man is not just a man because of his anatomy, but in how he handles a storm when it comes, and how he handles trouble and adversity when it comes.

A man thinks before
he speaks and is
slow to take action,
so he can make his
decisions from a
wise position.

Some people won't understand the grind until it's too late. The way to wealth is to have money working for you.

A leader's job is never done. Just stop and take a minute to think of your next ten moves.

Anger stops the
process of becoming
a great thinker.

The most attractive thing about a person is not the way they look, but how they handle pressure.

Don't be afraid to
be different, unique,
or one of a kind.
Don't follow, but
lead.

Some men get their
strength from the
sun; I get my
strength from God.

We hold ourselves back. It's not the people in office, it's not your career, it's not your kids or family. It's I, Me, Self.

Every day you should lay at least one brick toward building your empire. Don't leave just a name for your family, leave a legacy.

When life attacks,
stand your ground
and face it head on.

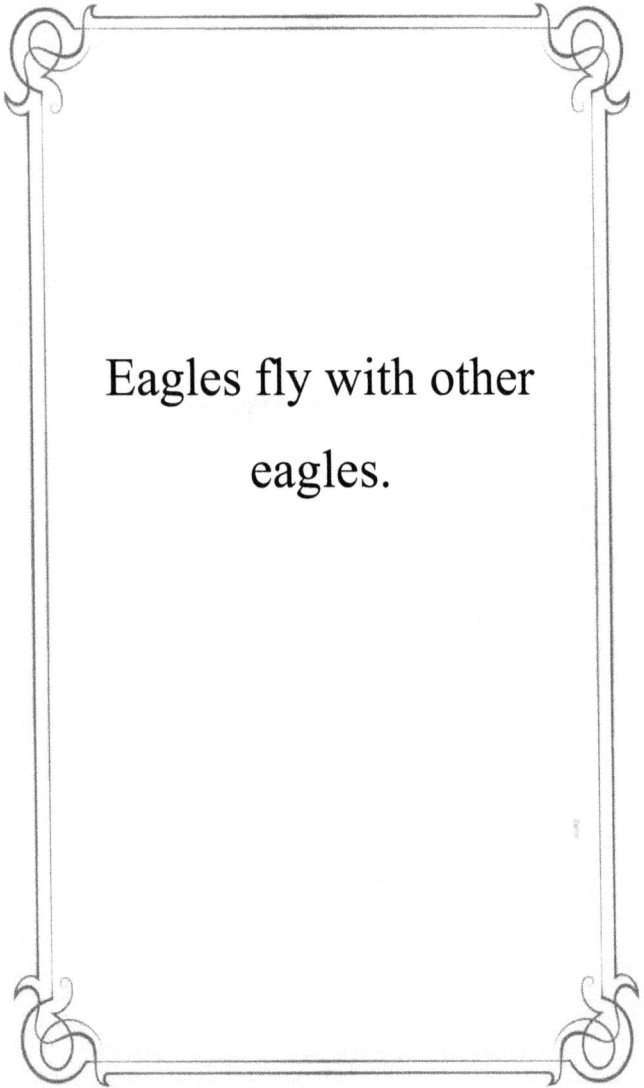

Eagles fly with other eagles.

Be fearless but wise. Have the courage to take risk, go where there are no guarantees, and get out of your comfort zone even if it means being uncomfortable. The road less traveled is sometimes blocked with barricades, bumps, and uncharted terrain. But it is on that road where your character is truly tested, and you have the courage to accept that you're not perfect.

It's not about how much money you make, it's about what you do with it. A millionaire can owe everyone and be broke, whereas someone working a minimum wage job could have no debt and be rich.

Stand your ground
and don't let life roll
over you.

Don't be afraid to walk against the norm. While everyone walks the same path as everyone else, choose to be different.

Sometimes you have to cut the weeds back and throw them away, in order to see the true beauty of the hidden flowers.

Action is everything.
Talk keeps you
paralyzed. Action
keeps you moving.

Rich men act broke.
Broke men act rich.
Which act are you?

Power under control is
more attractive than
just power.

A man who has never failed is a man who has never given it his all.

Make tomorrow be
the best day of the
rest of your life.

About the Author

Delorean Andrews was raised in the Liberty City neighborhood in Miami, FL. He is an aircraft electrician engineer. He is the founder of Release the Brakes, a non-profit organization helping young men of color foster self-confidence, community activism, and leadership for their future endeavors. He enjoys hiking, teaching financial literacy classes, horseback riding, rock climbing, and working on automobiles.

Follow him on social media:

@DeloreanAndrews on Facebook

@releasethebrakesdelorean Instagram

Email him at:
deloreandelorean2008@gmail.com

www.ingramcontent.com/pod-product-compliance
Lightning Source LLC
Chambersburg PA
CBHW051710090426
42736CB00013B/2636